Hands, Feet & Words Are Never – Ever for Hurting Others
A Workbook To Become Super Captain

Martie Morris Lee

I am Lady Arianna and I am Super Captain over my hands, feet and words. It's important to know that it's never – ever OK to use your hands and feet – or your words to hurt someone.

I'm an artist and I use my good hands for drawing.

Use your good hands to color my lily pad.

I am Sir Aiden and I am Super Captain over my hands, feet and words. It's important to know that it's never - ever OK to use your hands and feet -or your words to hurt someone.

Use your good hands to color my lily pad.

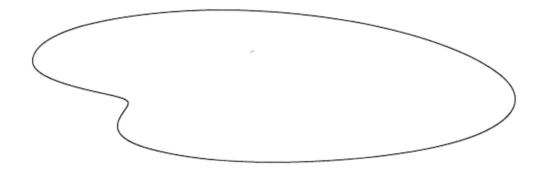

Hands & Feet Are Never – Ever for Hurting

Super Captains never hit, push or kick someone.

They never use their hands to grab toys away from someone.
They never use their hands to break someone's toys.

Put an X on all the faces that show frogs that are sad from being hurt.

Sir Aiden's friends are Super Captains over their
hands, feet and words. They look like they are
having fun using their good hands and feet.
Color the frogs in fun colors to show
frog happiness.

Sir Aiden is a Super Captain and he uses his hands to keep himself healthy.

Draw fun things that the frogs below could use in their good hands.

You use your good hands in many ways to take care of yourself.

Your hands hold soap to wash. Your hands hold a toothbrush to brush your teeth. Your hands also hold a brush or comb to do your hair.

On the lily pad, draw three items that you use to take care of yourself.

Super Captains use their good hands & feet in many ways to have fun.

Draw something that you really like to do using your hands or feet.

Use your good hands to color Lady Arianna's drawing that she made using her good hands.

You can use your good hands to play
musical instruments.

Draw a musical instrument that you would
like to play.

You can use your good feet to
dance to music.
You can use your good words to sing.

Help the frog find his way home to his
lily pad.

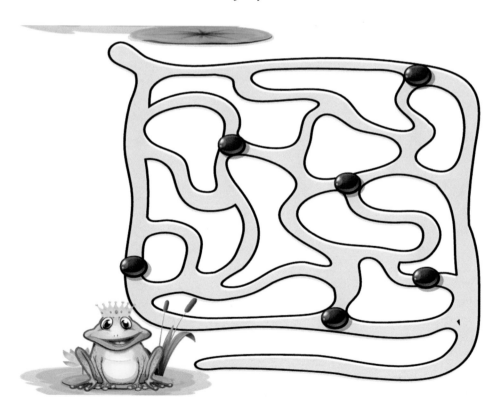

Super Captains use good words to:

Read a story

Talk

Talk to a friend

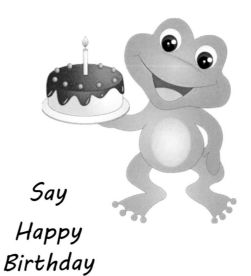

Say

Happy
Birthday

Words have power.
Some frogs use mean words to call others hurtful
names. Some use mean words to make fun
of others.
Super Captains never - ever call anyone hurtful
names. They do not make fun of others.
Super Captains use kind and respectful words.

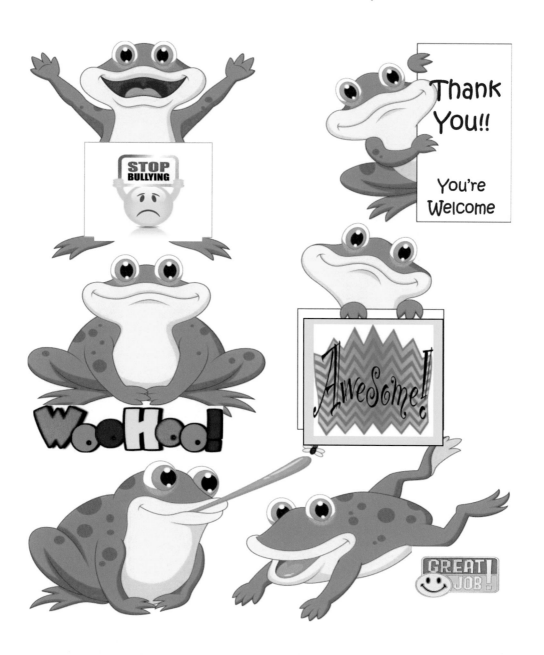

Circle the frogs that look happy from
hearing kind words.

Could you use your good hands to find a path for Timothy Turtle to find his way to his dinner?

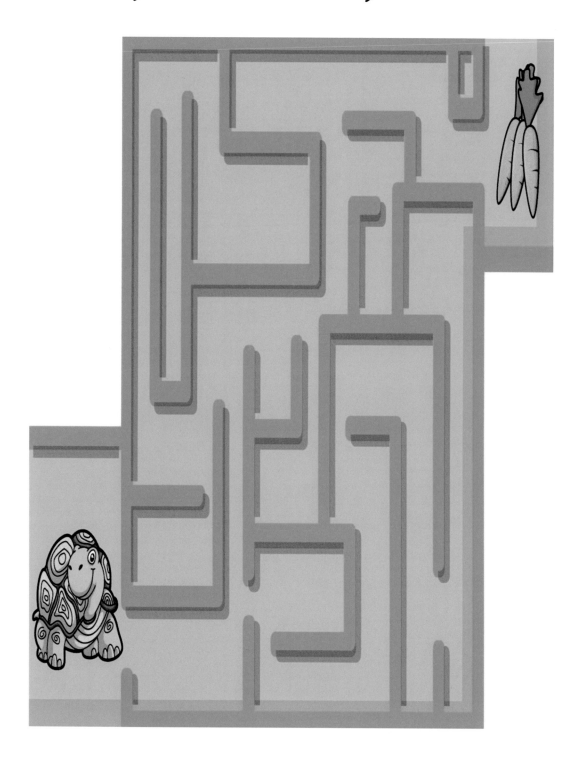

Some frogs use their hands, feet or words to bully others who are different than they are.

I became Super Captain over my hands, feet and words when I took a pledge to never — ever use them to hurt anyone.

I am a green frog. Circle all of my friends who are a different color than I am.

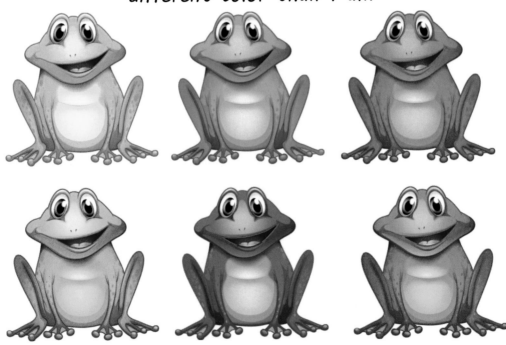

I have friends who are boys and girls and they became Super Captains. They took the pledge to never – ever use their hands, feet and words to hurt anyone.

They never – ever bully other boys and girls who are different than they are. They never hit, kick, push, or trip others. They never make fun of others who are different. They never use mean words to call them names.

These frogs and butterflies, along with the lizard,
beaver, dragon-fly, fish and turtle are
Super Captains.
They never - ever use their hands, feet, wings or
words to hurt each other.
They are all different and they respect each other.
They help each other. They have fun together.

Use your good hands to color their page.

Find the differences.

Kind words!

You have finished your workbook. You may sign the Super Captain pledge if you agree that it's never - ever OK to hurt someone by hitting, kicking, tripping, pushing, or by using hurtful words.

I pledge that I will not use my hands, feet or my words for hurting others. I am now a Super Captain.
My Name _____

I pledge that I will not use my hands, feet or my words for hurting others. I am now a Super Captain.
My Name _____

Martie Morris Lee
The workbooks and journals are for home use and also for use in groups, classrooms, organizations and agencies.

Workbooks for personal use and for classrooms

Capt'n Jack's Personal Power Workbook: To Become Super Capt'n of Self-Control (Boys & Girls, Grades 2-6)

Capt'n Jane's Impulse Control Workbook: Self-Talk, Self-Control, Coping Skills (Boys & Girls Grades, 2-4)

Stop Bullying – The Power of One Workbook (Boys & Girls, Grades 1-3)

Your Hands, Feet & Words Are Never – Ever for Hurting Others: A Workbook To Become Super Captain (Boys & Girls, Grades Pre-School-1)

Timothy Turtle's Special Techniques: Workbook for Impulse Control (Boys & Girls, Grades 1- 3)

Your Journey to Personal Power Workbook (Teen Girls)

Personal Power... for Guys (Teens)

Positively Empowered! (Women)

Life Coaching Journals for personal use and for classroom and individual/agency activities

My Dance... My Journey Journal for Women (Life Coaching)

Life Coaching Journal for Teen Girls

Life Coaching Journal for 'Tween Girls

Life Coaching Journal for Teen Guys

Life Coaching Journal for Men

Prior to becoming a certified life coach, Martie Lee spent 20 years as an executive director of a non-profit that is in the business of empowering women, teens, 'tweens and children and she developed several youth personal development programs.

Find the hidden frog and color the page with your good hands.

Find 5 differences

Made in the USA
Lexington, KY
16 October 2017